THE KING

OF

CRIPPLE CREEK

EDITORIAL NOTE

The King of Cripple Creek was first published in 1953 in *"True Magazine"* as a book-length feature. Many standards used in copy editing have evolved in the intervening four decades. We have chosen to leave the manuscript in its form of the 1950s. This retains the delightful storytelling style of Marshall Sprague, who in this work of fiction, captured the flavor of Colorado in the day of *The King of Cripple Creek.*

©1994 by Magazine Associates
Reprinted by permission. First appeared in *True,* March 1953.

ISBN 1-884003-04-4 paperbound

NOTE OF THANKS

The friends of the Pikes Peak Library District express sincere thanks to Betty Clausen, distinguished Colorado Springs bookseller, for bringing to our attention this important piece by Marshall Sprague; to Adrian B. Lopez, president of Magazine Associates for granting kind permission to publish this book; to Jeanette Bogren for her excellent skills in typesetting and typography; to the Friends Committee: Andrea Corley, Ken Hallenbeck, Anne Moreland, and Jim Bixler; and library Director Bernie Margolis, along with library staff members Ree Mobley, Mary Mashburn and Nancy Downs, who worked to see this project to successful completion.

The Friends
of the
Pikes Peak Library District

Andrea Corley
President

Joyce Small	Jimmie Butler	Anna-Leah Hathaway
Mary Lou Sieben	Bliss Eckland	David Kuamoo
Martin Zelinsky	Betty Francis	Lillian Mallory
Rosemae Campbell	Karen Gilmer	Anne Moreland
Lois Crouch	Jerold Greenker	Joy Perry
Doris Adams	Ken Hallenbeck	Charles Robinove
Art Argenzio	Dottie Harman	Darnell Rucker
James Bixler	Kay Wells	Polly Wells

Many regard Marshall Sprague as the premier historian of the Pikes Peak Region. He seems to have been chosen by fate—and well-prepared by education and experience—for that role. Born in Newark, Ohio in 1909, he attended the Lawrenceville School and Princeton University. After working as a reporter in New York, Sprague served a year on the *North China Star* in Tientsin and on the Paris edition of the *New York Herald Tribune*. In 1941 Sprague came to Colorado Springs to recover from tuberculosis. While he regained his health he discovered the people and events that demanded his talents as writer and historian. For many years he contributed to numerous magazines and has been a feature writer for the *New York Times*. His works have won awards from the Colorado Authors' League, a Pulitzer Prize nomination in history, and Colorado College's Benjamin McKie Rastall Award for "distinguished service to the cultural development of Colorado." Marshall Sprague was married to Edna Jane Ailes and they had three children. He died September 9, 1994 in Colorado Springs, Colorado.

Marshall Sprague, 1953, Publicity Portrait publication of *Money Mountain: The Story of Cripple Creek Gold.*

—Knutson-Bowers Studio

THE KING

OF

CRIPPLE CREEK

The Life and Times

of

Winfield Scott Stratton,

First Millionaire

from the

Cripple Creek Gold Strike

FRIENDS

OF THE

PIKES PEAK LIBRARY DISTRICT

Colorado Springs, Colorado

BOOKS BY MARSHALL SPRAGUE

The Business of Getting Well 1942

Money Mountain: The Story of Cripple Creek Gold 1953

Massacre: The Tragedy at White River 1957

*Newport in the Rockies: The Life and Good Times
of Colorado Springs* 1961

*The Great Gates: The Story of the
Rocky Mountain Passes* 1964

*The Mountain States:
Arizona, Colorado, Idaho, Montana* 1967

A Gallery of Dudes 1967

*One Hundred Plus: A Centennial Story of
Colorado Springs* 1971

First Century at the First 1973

*So Vast, So Beautiful a Land:
Louisiana and the Purchase* 1974

Colorado: A Bicentennial History 1976

El Paso Club: A Century of Friendship 1976

Grizzlies: A History of the Cheyenne Mountain Zoo 1983

Colorado: A History 1984

Greetings from Colorado 1988

*Chinook: A Promise of Spring: Thirty Years of
Bookselling on Tejon Street, 1959-1989* 1989

FOREWORD

Today the evidence of both the wealth and caring of the real *King of Cripple Creek,* Winfield Scott Stratton, is seen throughout Colorado Springs. Winfield Scott Stratton was the first millionaire to make his fortune from the gold strike at Cripple Creek. In his time, the titles of *Midas of the Rockies, Winfield Scott the Great,* and *The King of Cripple Creek* all were appropriate descriptions of the man who made a significant mark upon what was then called "Little London:" and is now affectionately called "the Springs."

Stratton, born on July 22, 1848 in Jeffersonville, Indiana, was named after General Winfield Scott, who was distinguished for his military career in the Spanish American war. From his Midwest beginnings as a carpenter, Stratton brought his skills to Colorado Springs in 1871, where he later invested in real estate and mining. Most of his first mining ventures failed, as did his marriage, and Stratton found himself again in the carpentry business. His interest and attraction to the mining enterprise was so great that he studied metallurgy and geology at both The Colorado College and the Colorado School of Mines. The year 1891 found him back in Cripple Creek where, on the fourth of July, he staked two claims on Battle Mountain. His wealth was almost instantaneous; the two claims revealed a rich vein of gold which produced millions of dollars in short order.

Soon after the successful gold strike, Stratton began to reveal his philanthropic disposition. Various accounts talk of his largesse to the Salvation Army, which used $85,000 given by Stratton to provide meals and rooms to homeless miners in Cripple Creek. His generosity even extended to providing some medical benefits to those who worked in the many mines he owned and operated in Cripple Creek.

Throughout his life, Stratton was known for his reclusive ways. Rather than hobnobbing with the rich and famous of his time, he was known as the friend of the working person. Stratton was more comfortable with miners, servants, and boot makers than with the upper strata of Colorado Springs society.

Today, the most visible continuing evidence of Stratton's generosity is found at the Myron Stratton Home. Named after Stratton's father, the home opened in 1913—almost a dozen years after Stratton's death. Lawsuits and challenges, including those of dozens of women—all of whom insisted they had been married to Stratton, had delayed Stratton's dream of using his $15 million fortune to support the common people who had meant so much to him during his life. Today, more than 80 years later, the Myron Stratton Home continues to provide for those in need.

The King of Cripple Creek is a fictional account of Cripple Creek in the 1890s by Marshall Sprague, beloved Colorado Springs author who has been an important chronicler of the history of our region. In *Money Mountain, Newport in the Rockies, Cheyenne Mountain Ranch,* and other works by Marshall Sprague, the colorful history of our region has been documented.

Marshall Sprague's gift for storytelling is evident in *The King of Cripple Creek.* In presenting it, the author's intent is to provide a glimpse of Cripple Creek in its heyday, not to make any judgment about whether Winfield Scott Stratton was a saint or sinner. "Barking dealers, singing drunks, laughing girls, yelling waiters" were no doubt part of the culture of Cripple Creek in the 1890s. Some think that one hundred years later they have all returned!

Also characteristic of the day was litigation pitting one miner and his claim against another with investors and speculators jumping into the litigation fray at every turn. Marshall Sprague, no doubt, has embellished the story and dialogue to bring us the picture of the excitement of gold in Cripple Creek. He weaves the story of Winfield Scott Stratton, a man to whom he attributes great intellect, and the excitement of the wheeling and dealing common to our history then— and maybe even now.

Reading *The King of Cripple Creek* will ensure that any visit to Cripple Creek today will bring to mind a town of people with gold fever. Imagine the excitement of wagons, people, and horses crowding into the streets, as you run to the assay office with a bag of new-found gold ore.

Please enjoy this story. Its happy ending, noting the creation of the Myron Stratton Home, gives Winfield Scott Stratton the title of "The King of Cripple Creek" and the appropriate designation of "patron of the poor."

Bernard A. Margolis
Director
Pikes Peak Library District

On a blazing afternoon like this, Jimmy Burns wished he were home in Colorado Springs fixing drains. His arms ached from cranking up waste rock which his partner Jimmy Doyle was mucking down in the Portland mine. Doyle was a husky youngster. It was cool where he was. But Jimmy Burns was 43 years old. He was a sparrow of a man. His lungs hurt in that Alpine altitude. Sweat trickled down his pink face from the roots of his white hair. All around him on this hot hill and on other Cripple Creek hills he could see swarms of tenderfeet like himself scratching for gold. Not far above him to the northeast was the brown top of Pikes Peak where tourists were sipping cool lemon squash in the Summit House. To the west was the Continental Divide. But the view Jimmy liked best was to the south, the snow-streaked Sangre de Cristos. Their lacelike spires made him think of the ruffles on Georgia Hayden's drawers.

At least he had Georgia to look forward to. Soon he'd be off Battle Mountain and out of these stinking clothes. He would wash in Wilson Creek near the Burns-Doyle shack. He would put on his pin-stripe and wing collar like the clothes the English actors wore in *Charlie's Aunt*. And then he would be at Johnny Nolon's, drinking beer with Georgia. He had something to ask her tonight. Maybe she would, maybe not. If only he could tell her the truth about the Portland!

He cranked the last bucket to the top of the rickety windlass. Out of it jumped Jimmy Doyle, the damn fool. Suppose the rope had broken? But that was Doyle for you. At the mine he handled dynamite like stick candy. At the shack down the hill he seldom washed a dish, made a bed, swept the floor or carried a pail of water. He was a great joker. One night he brought home a load of giddy girls from the red end of Poverty Gulch. One of them was Hook-and-Ladder Kate. She was the largest prostitute in Colorado. When Burns tried to drive her away she took him in her arms, removed his nightgown and spanked his bottom.

Doyle laughed and laughed.

And still Burns loved Doyle like a son. Both men were red-neck Irish Catholics and red necks had to stick together. Furthermore, Burns owed Doyle the chance of his life. Doyle had located the Portland, and gave Burns half of it. Burns knew now that the Portland was a gold mine. A great gold mine—perhaps the richest in Cripple Creek. Hadn't Burns and Doyle carried out secretly more than $80,000 worth of high-grade? And wasn't that high-grade less than a tenth of the rich stuff which lay exposed in the first level? And wouldn't they find millions more along the big vein if they dared to develop the Portland openly?

That was the catch. Normal lode claims at Cripple were 1,500 feet long by 300 feet wide—about ten acres. The Portland was smaller than your backyard. Old Man Stratton had spotted the trouble months ago. Burns had led him up to the claim to ask where to start digging. Stratton had glanced at the patch of ragged hillside. Then he had said, "Forget it, boys." Burns had asked, "What d'you mean, Mr. Stratton?" The tall, thin prospector had pointed to the stakes of many earlier claims pressing in on the Portland. "You have thirty prior claims here," Stratton had said. "If you hit good ore, every owner around will sue you, claiming you are on his vein. That's the law of apex."

The law of apex stated that a vein belonged to the claim on which it surfaced even though that vein might run far beyond the boundaries of the claim. As far as Burns and Doyle knew, no vein apexed on the Portland. They dug anyhow. They took in John Harnan, another red neck. It was Harnan who recognized the big gold vein thirty feet down. No apex. The vein just ran through their ground. They remembered Stratton's warning. They didn't tell a soul.

Harnan didn't work very much. He was the professional adviser. Burns and Doyle took turns carrying out the sacked high-grade by night. They hid it under Burns' bed. Once a week one of them carted the sacks down the awful shelf road to Canon City and on to the Pueblo smelter. Each sack averaged 25 ounces of gold. Gold brought $20 an ounce.

So Burns was making $150 a day. That's what

he wanted to tell Georgia Hayden when he got spruced up and met her in one of the dark booths of the wine room at Johnny Nolon's. Technically, Georgia wasn't a sporting woman, though she smoked cigarettes, lived on Myers Avenue and took meals at Crapper Jack's. She was one of several smart girls who had picked up some capital as rotating mistresses in Leadville and Creede. They had come to Cripple to find more men with money. Lately Burns had grown fond of Georgia. And he liked the look of her tonight. She had a stimulating plumpness. The low bodice of her shirtwaist only half hid her breasts. She had careless blonde curls framed by a black straw hat. Jimmy liked the feel of her hand on his leg as they sat chatting or listening to the click of billiard balls and the different click of the roulette wheel. From the bar came the smell of beer and cheese.

Burns put his arm around Georgia and asked her to marry him. Her eyes opened wide. Then she giggled. She told him amiably not to be silly. She hadn't come up to Cripple to marry a $3-a-day plumber, even if he was a tidy, clean, smart fellow who dressed snappy. She was a rich man's woman. On the other hand, if Jimmy should happen to find $10,000 in that mine of his, Georgia would be happy to move in with him.

Jimmy just did manage to control himself. The Portland had earned him twice $10,000 already! But he knew that to tell Georgia would be the same as telling every one of the 12,000 souls who were crawling over Cripple like ants on an ant hill. Then the Battle Mountain boys with claims near the tiny Portland would file injunctions. Sheriff Bowers would come puffing up Battle and would order the Irishmen out of their own mine. The law of apex.

So Jimmy did not tell Georgia the secret. To ease his frustration, he yelled for a double whisky. He drank it, slammed on his derby and left Georgia. Outside Nolon's he mounted his horse and let the animal pick its way down Third Street through the mob of men and women who kept traffic roaring between the Bennett Avenue saloons and the wide-open sin belt of Myers Avenue. As Burns left town on the Battle Mountain road, the din of dance-hall pianos faded. He stopped at a Squaw Gulch saloon for a drink, passed over Guyot Hill and around Squaw Mountain and on to the Burns-Doyle shack. The place was a mess. It was Doyle's day to clean up. The dishes were unwashed. A pair of female garters lay right in the middle of the floor. No Doyle.

Fuming, Burns drank two more whiskies. He changed from his new suit into his hated work clothes. He picked up his ore sack and scrambled up the steep hill past Sam Strong's shaft, past Old Man Stratton's well-built cabin and his Independence Mine and across the intervening claims to the Portland. He sat a bit to catch his breath and to swig from his bottle before hefting the high-grade sack into the harness. He struggled to his feet with the sack on his back and reeled down the hill again. He was dizzy. Suddenly he fell. The fall didn't hurt him, but he was pinned down by the sack and harness. He flailed his wiry arms and legs for some minutes. Then he started cussing. He was good at it. His high-pitched words covered most of man's abnormalities. They flew to Big Bull Mountain and bounced back furiously.

Old Winfield Scott Stratton heard the racket. He was charting his Independence Mine in his cabin. He laid down his T-square, lit his lantern and moved calmly toward Burns. He didn't have far to go. He cut Burns free and led him back to his cabin. He gave him a drink. While Burns sat recovering, Stratton squinted through his magnifying glass at a piece of high-grade from Burns' sack. He saw at once that it was excellent ore. He muttered, "Well, I'll be damned." He faced Jimmy and waited.

Burns finished his whisky and put down his glass. He stared bleary-eyed at Stratton. Gradually the old man came into focus. Then Burns saw the gleam in Stratton's pale blue eyes, usually expressionless like the glass eyes of a doll. Stratton knew now about the Portland. No use trying to fool him. Burns began to talk. He told Stratton everything there was to tell.

Jimmy had always admired and trusted the old man. He had known him for years in Colorado Springs where Stratton was a carpenter who prospected during the summers. Stratton wasn't really old. He was only two years older than Burns himself. But Burns looked young, in spite of his pure white hair. Stratton looked ancient, patriarchal. His weathered face had the pallor of weariness. His white handlebar mustache drooped. His tall, thin body was as stooped as Father Time's.

He was born in 1848 at Jeffersonville, Indiana, the son of an Ohio river-boat builder, Myron Stratton. Myron named him after General Winfield Scott because that was the fashion when "Old Fuss and Feathers" was riding the crest of his Mexican War wave. Myron was a nagger. He made Winfield so angry one day that the boy grabbed his rifle and took a shot at his father. He missed. Many years later he gave millions in his father's memory to atone for his attempted patricide.

Young Stratton's mother was a smothering female who produced one girl baby after another. She had eight girls all told. The boy grew up changing girls' diapers. By the time he was 10 he was so sick of females that he decided to have nothing more to do with women. Those were great days. If you didn't like home you packed up and went West. At 20, Stratton visited relatives in Iowa where a phrenologist examined his head and advised him to be an undertaker. He moved on to Nebraska and, in 1872, to Colorado Springs.

General William J. Palmer had founded the town the year before at the foot of Pikes Peak. Even then it was nicknamed "Little London" because of its English mood and tempo. Palmer had planned it as a haven for rich invalids, retired capitalists and young members of Eastern society yearning for romance on horseback. The place hasn't changed much.

Myron Stratton had taught his son carpentry. Winfield was glad to have this trade when he reached Little London. He set up shop on Pikes Peak Avenue and soon had more work than he could handle. He was a fine organizer, a sound and imaginative builder, an honest craftsman. He taught himself higher mathematics and this helped him to make accurate estimates on big jobs in a few minutes.

But he had unstable impulses. By May of 1874, three of his business partnerships had ended in fights. He quit carpentry for awhile and sank $2,800 of real-estate profits into a mining claim in the San Juan range of the Rockies. He spent two months on this claim, learning the facts of mining life. The facts in this case were easy to learn. He lost $2,800. And yet he was not unhappy about it. He had discovered that the hunting for gold fitted his temperament. The quest gave him excitement without the vexations which he encountered building houses. He was soothed by the placid aloofness of the mountains, the pleasant sound of mountain streams, the simple way things were put together. He liked the smell of sage after rain and the gray-green of aspens in a summer breeze. He liked traveling with a burro. Burros did not talk back, quibble, complain, belittle, overcharge, or boast of their virility. They just did what they were told to do without jawbone.

For seventeen summers the quest for gold was Stratton's absorbing passion. In the winter he built houses and did cabinet work in Little London. He got off the beam only once. In March of '76, a 17-year-old girl named Zeurah Stewart came to stay at Stratton's boardinghouse. She was pretty, slim, agreeable and homesick for her native Illinois. One evening on the porch she came to Stratton's arms for comforting. He liked the sensation. He began to revise his views on women. Zeurah's soft kisses made him wonder if prospecting was so much fun after all. Maybe he needed a wife, children, a home. Once Stratton asked for more than kisses, but Zeurah shyly turned him down.

That happened in June. On their wedding night Zeurah told Stratton that she was three-months pregnant. She added that she was telling her friends that Stratton was the child's father. Stratton recalled seeing Zeurah a time or two with a bartender at the Antlers Hotel. He exploded. He pushed Zeurah from their room in her nightgown. He tossed her clothes after her. Next morning he bought her rail ticket and put her on the train bound for Illinois. Her baby, a boy, was born six months later. Stratton never saw Zeurah again and he got a divorce in 1879.

The carpenter got around in the 80's. He plodded across the lovely treeless plateau of South Park and prospected Chalk Creek below Mount Princeton.

He combed the slatey gulches near Granite, curried Baker's Park in the San Juans and hurried to Leadville, the world's greatest silver camp. He found nothing, though Horace Tabor, Leadville's king, paid him well to make a cedar chest for his mistress, Baby Doe. Stratton tried the Blue River country, swung south to Rosita in the Wet Mountain Valley and north again to the Elk Mountains, Aspen and Red Cliff.

He became as mountain-wise as Kit Carson. He learned to be comfortable in all weathers. He felt at home anywhere in the Colorado Rockies. He became a full-fledged member of the prospecting breed—fearless men driven to find the seldom findable. These were the men who opened the American West, and most other remote places for that matter. The Colorado species had faces cracked by wind, hail and rain. They shaved rarely, wore shabby felt hats, ragged shirts, patched pants, heavy shoes. They were expert hunters and anglers. They chewed tobacco, drank incredible quantities of cheap whisky and lived on beans, pork and hope. Most of them were uneducated, guided more by superstition than by science. Perhaps that is why everything worth finding was found by them, instead of by the mining engineers who held them in such scorn. Gold is where you find it, not where it ought to be.

But Winfield Stratton wasn't an ordinary prospector. He had intellect. He had a thirst to learn. He studied the nature of ores in the Nashold mill at Breckenridge. He learned blowpipe analysis at Colorado College. He studied geology at the Colorado School of Mines where he crossed a spot daily to be occupied later by a laboratory building called Stratton Hall. And still he failed to strike it rich. In the spring of '91 he turned away from gold to hunt such humdrum minerals around Pikes Peak as potash and cryolite. One day a prospecting friend of his, Bob Womack, stopped him on Pikes Peak Avenue. Bob was one of the best cowboys in El Paso County. People claimed that he once rode his horse safely up the stairs of Blanche Barton's parlor house in Colorado City. They claimed that he could lean from his saddle and snatch a bottle of bourbon from the ground with his teeth.

W omack started raving to Stratton about a place called Cripple Creek. He was, as usual, half crocked. Stratton had heard the same yarn periodically for a dozen years. Womack was always about to find gold. This time, he insisted, he really had a mine in Poverty Gulch. A bunch of fellows were there already. Others were going up at the rate of five or six a day. Stratton ought to look Cripple Creek over.

Stratton shrugged. He told Womack he'd think about it, but he knew there could be no gold at Cripple. It was nothing but a cow pasture. It was just on the other side of Pikes Peak, only 18 miles as the crow flies from Colorado Springs. Prospectors by the hundreds had walked over it in the past thirty years. Major Demary, a famous South Park mining engineer, had a fishing shack right in the middle of Cripple's low hills. If Cripple had gold, Demary of all people would know it. Demary called Womack "Crazy Bob."

When Stratton shook Bob off, he went to the volunteer fire station above the Springs city hall to watch a checker game. These volunteer fire companies were like the service clubs of today. They gave parties and held benefits and worked at politics and made themselves generally useful. The one thing they did not do very well was fight fires. Buildings sometimes burned to the ground while the rival companies scrapped with one another. Stratton learned that Womack had been at the city hall fire station and had talked to three amateur firemen. Jimmy Burns, Jimmy Doyle and the roustabout, Sam Strong. They were all fired up about Cripple. Especially the little plumber, Burns. Stratton watching him spewing words in his high voice. Burns tickled him. Perhaps it was Burns' zest, his sure grasp of what he wanted, his bright illusions. Burns intended to go places. He watched his chances. He was as careful of his appearance as a pretty girl. He kept his boots shined. He kept shaved. He kept his prematurely white hair parted neatly.

Leslie Popejoy, a plasterer, entered the fire station. He listened to Burns for quite a spell. Then he asked Stratton to investigate Cripple for him. He offered him a grubstake of $275. Stratton accepted it. Next day he packed his burro and went up through the green forest over Cheyenne Mountain around the south side of Pikes Peak to Poverty Gulch. Cripple seemed to him even more unpromising than he had expected with its bleak hills covered with blue-gray turf and scattered aspen. Spruce groves spilled down the gulches. He noticed only a few granite outcrops and no quartz formations. At Poverty he found a shivering bunch of tenderfeet scratching like chickens. They had come up because the April business slump in Little London had put them out of their usual work of clerking or painting or butchering or coddling millionaires. They didn't know what a gold mine looked like or how to build a fire or stake a tent or handle a burro. One old-timer complained to Stratton, "Maybe they got sense enough to keep their pants buttoned in a blizzard. I am mean enough to doubt that statement."

Stratton saw nothing to Poverty Gulch. The ignorance of the tenderfeet depressed him. He drifted south over Gold Hill and Raven Hill and Squaw Mountain to a crooked hill of 500 acres which Womack called Battle Mountain. It was about 500 feet high. No tenderfeet here. Stratton watered his burro in Wilson Creek. Just above it on Battle's south slope he raised his tent near a granite outcrop. He slept well that night under what looked to him like all the stars in the universe.

Early next morning, as he enjoyed a tender-foot-free breakfast, he heard gravel rattling up the slope. Three heads appeared over the ridge. Three grinning men marched down toward him. They raised three tents in a line below his. Two were volunteer firemen—his checker players. The third was the roust-about, Sam Strong. At noon, a fourth tenderfoot arrived and raised his tent—Jimmy Burns. His first act was to bathe in the creek and change his clothes. He told Stratton that Jimmy Doyle would join him soon.

There were five tents on Battle now. Stratton had a strong urge to flee the crowd, but he stayed for weeks. He located a dozen claims, most of which he gave to the tenderfeet. Early in June he packed up and returned to Colorado Springs. But he dreamed of Battle Mountain. He dreamed of that lonely granite outcrop near where his tent had been. He had tested it once with his blowpipe and crucible and there had been no trace of gold. An yet it was peculiar. Stratton went through his whole prospecting experience to find an explanation. He thought of Cripple's volcanic structure and of its geological career—and then he had an idea.

Perhaps the granite outcrop marked the outer edge of an ancient volcano. If so, a good-sized vein might exist along its face underground. Such veins were common at the perimeters of volcanos. A contact vein of this kind might contain a rich filling of gold.

The carpenter with his burro hurried back up the old Cheyenne Mountain trail to Wilson Creek. The granite outcrop was still unclaimed. On July 4, 1891, Stratton staked the ground around it. He called his claim the Independence. He began sinking a shaft and he hit a smattering of gold a few feet below the dirt overwash. This vein assayed poorly, though values improved some with depth. However, he was broke by September. His grubstaker, Leslie Popejoy, refused further support. Stratton went to Sam Altman, the Squaw Gulch saw-mill man, for a loan. Sam took him to Blanch Barton who had closed her Colorado City parlor house and had opened another at Cripple in a tent borrowed from an evangelist. The tent was pitched up the slope in Poverty Gulch so the customers wouldn't be washed out by flash floods.

Blanche loaned Altman and Stratton $950. Then she asked Stratton a question. Tim Hussey called on her often and paid her each time by giving her an eighth interest in his Prince Albert mine. She had twenty-seven eighths altogether. How much of the Prince Albert belonged to her now? Stratton spent Blanche's $950 paying Popejoy and settling small accounts with Burns, Doyle, Sam Strong and other tenderfeet who had helped him at times.

From July of '91 to June of '93 Stratton toiled on the Independence. He didn't know why. The fool mine would barely earn him beans for months and then would present him with a pay streak worth several hundred dollars. He found many small veins.

But the big contact vein which he had visualized eluded him. When he found it at last it was under circumstances that made him wish he hadn't.

He found it when he had just signed the Independence over to a San Francisco speculator, L.M. Pearlman, for $5,000 on a thirty-day option. Stratton had deposited Pearlman's check in the Bi-Metallic Bank and had returned to the mine to get his tools. The Independence shaft was 85 feet deep. It had four crosscuts at the 50-foot level. Stratton removed his equipment from three of them. He had abandoned the fourth crosscut in '92 and it occurred to him to check that one, too. He wormed his way in through the debris and found a rusty drill. He poked it into the wall and a loose rock fell. Behind it was the purplish discoloration which marked the outer edge of a thick telluride vein tinted with fluoride. Stratton kept poking. In an hour he had established the scope and trend of the vein.

When he left the crosscut he tried to replace the debris. Maybe Pearlman wouldn't investigate this crosscut. It was a slim chance. Stratton went to his cabin sick at heart. He made assays of samples from the big vein. They showed $380 a ton laterally for 27 feet. The vein had to be at least 9 feet wide, 100 feet deep. That meant $3,000,000 worth of gold ore in sight!

Here was the end of his quest. Here was his pot of gold at the end of the rainbow which he had been chasing since '74. And Pearlman would get it all if he exercised his option within thirty days.

That night Stratton emptied two quarts of whisky rapidly and fell asleep across his table.

It was exactly a week later that Stratton responded to Jimmy Burns' caterwauling and cut the squirming plumber loose from his ore-sack harness. Stratton had good reason to listen to Burns' tale of the Portland's secret wealth. As Burns rattled on, Stratton became convinced that the Portland vein and the Independence vein were the same vein. The Portland claim was near the top of Battle Mountain. The Independence was near the bottom. Therefore that big vein had to pass through several hundred yards of claims between the Portland and the Independence.

Stratton's mine had $3,000,000 worth of gold ore in sight. Burn's Portland was so rich that three small Irishmen had carried out on their backs high-grade ore worth $80,000.

Burns asked Stratton if $80,000 was enough to fight the apex suits that were sure to develop. Stratton said no. Then he told Burns about the Independence vein. He sketched its probable extent through the Portland and beyond. He said, "Jimmy, you fellows can't fight those suits alone. You need me. Our two mines hold the key to Cripple. Between them we can lick every jaw-bone lawyer in Colorado. And we'll buy Battle Mountain."

Next morning Burns had a session with Jimmy Doyle and John Harnan. Then the three Irishmen called on Stratton. They talked strategy. All agreed that Stratton should direct the Portland's defense. They shook hands and the deal was on. There were no papers, no precise commitments. It was just a mutual-assistance pact between friends.

The first problem was Pearlman's option on the Independence. The option had twenty-two days to run. Stratton knew that Pearlman was having trouble hiring an exploration crew. Harnan collected the Houghton boys and other friends and offered Pearlman a complete crew. Pearlman was delighted. Harnan put the crew to blasting in the main drift, heading into the granite where values were low. Pearlman was not suspicious. He knew nothing about gold mining, but he was a nuisance. He pottered around in the Independence. He kept pestering Stratton for advice and it made Stratton nervous.

One night Stratton decided to relax. Cripple was a wonderful place for it. The town was even less inhibited than Leadville at its most prosperous. Things had been slow in '91 and '92. But in '93 Cripple's population had reached a fantastic figure. The reason was the depression throughout the world. People flocked to Cripple to share in its prosperity. Four six-horse stages clattered daily down Mount Pisgah's slopes from Florissant to the Palace Hotel. Four more arrived from the Divide rail depot. Another clambered up from Canon City. A tenth took the Cheyenne Mountain road from Little London.

E very kind of human stepped from these stages at the long Palace porch—pompous English lords, French barons, great engineers in high boots, well-heeled youngsters out of Harvard; dignified madames in black silk and giggling dance-hall girls in short frocks, their muscular legs exposed. The high-priced sporting ladies rode atop the stages to display their Paris dresses and tight-laced figures. Gentlemen were always on hand to help them as they stepped down, their dresses lifted genteelly to show their red pantalettes. Some of these ladies couldn't speak English. They were Russian, perhaps from the bordellos of Shanghai and Tientsin, or French girls from Montmartre. One day seven tiny Japanese in brilliant kimonos stepped from the stage and minced down Third Street to quarters next to the Red Light Dance Hall.

At first Cripple's tenderloin was on Bennett Avenue among the groceries, meat markets, barber shops, bathhouses and mush-and-milk joints. But affairs got so confused that Marshall Hi Wilson moved the girls and dance halls a block south to

Myers Avenue between Fifth and Third Street. Everyone respected Wilson. He wasn't the old-style hip-shootin' sort of sheriff. He would simply walk up to you and take away your gun. "We don't allow them things up here, bub," He would say. "I'll just sell this for the school fund." Hi controlled the population of prostitutes and collected a head tax of a dollar a day. Some of the head tax went to Cripple's churches. Some went to Dr. Whiting and Dr. Hereford who helped control venereal disease.

Cripple's early dance halls, parlor houses and cribs were built overnight of green lumber and were lined inside with heavy muslin. There were class distinctions. The quality of sin was better and costlier on Myers near Third Street. It lost glamor as it moved east toward Poverty Gulch. The cribs, starting at Myers and Fourth, were one-story shacks, each occupied by an older woman unable to make the parlor-house grade. These free-lancers solicited in the nude before their street windows, using the blind as a teaser. The worst houses, pure brutality and lust, began east of Fifth and ran for some yards into Poverty Gulch.

So Winfield Stratton guided his burro toward Myers Avenue to relax and forget about Pearlman's option on the Independence. As he crossed Raven Hill he marveled at how things had changed since the day Jimmy Burns and Sam Strong had shattered his Battle Mountain peace. The old path was a highway now, almost a street. There were buildings all along—miners' shacks, shaft houses, stores, saloons. Even after dark the road was alive with people. He passed through two bustling villages, Elkton and Anaconda.

And what, Stratton asked himself, had transformed this Alpine pasture into one of the most frenetic centers of human activity on earth? The answer was greed for gold. And what caused the greed? He couldn't say. He only knew that gold, like sex, was something everyone has yearned for since Adam and Eve, without knowing precisely why. Didn't the Bible imply that God made gold even before He made sex? Gold was mentioned in the twelfth verse of the second chapter of Genesis. Adam and Eve came in several verses later.

Business was good on Myers Avenue. Stratton saw that the crib blinds were all down. He hitched his burro at the Butte Opera House and strolled westward on Myers. At Fourth Street a crowd cheered a frowsy blonde in a petticoat who sat on the chest of a skinny man beating his face. He had tried to jump his bill. A landau swept by. A fiddler sawed away on the box beside the driver. Five ladies rode in the landau, their bare arms holding their great hats in place. Stratton watched the landau stop at Lola Livingston's where the ladies swept grandly inside. Near Third Street, Stratton entered Crapper Jack's. The din split his eardrums—band, barking dealers, singing drunks, laughing girls, yelling waiters. The sawdust floor was wet with spilled beer. Stratton had a whisky. He grabbed the nearest girl and led her to the dance floor. He gathered her in his arms but he was badly coordinated as a dancer. He had scarcely started before the caller shouted, "Promenade to the bar!" For this brief dance Stratton paid 25 cents.

He left Crapper Jack's soon. He stopped at the Bucket of Blood and the Red Onion and the Topic, a great barn with a variety stage at one end. It had a second-story gallery with tables. Stratton saw Jimmy Burns and Georgia Hayden up there watching some girl acrobats on the variety stage. He had a drink with them. Then Candace Root passed by and took the next table. He joined her.

Candace was a sweet-faced brunette with brown eyes and an air of gentle confusion. She worked off and on at Hazel Vernon's, Cripple's most distinguished parlor house. Stratton had drawn the plans for Candace's little shack on Warren Avenue and he had built a frame for her sewing machine. He had even saved her life one snowy night when he had noticed an odd pile of snow in the lot behind the Central Dance Hall. He had brushed off the snow. Underneath was Candace, dead drunk and clad in her thin dance-hall frock. He had thrown her over his shoulder, hurried to her home, heated water, bathed her, rubbed her until her pulse was more normal and put her to bed under warm blankets. He left her an envelope containing $200 and a note urging her to take the Keeley cure in Denver—injections of bichloride of gold plus a diet of raw carrots. Candace had eaten carrots for six weeks and then had returned to Cripple to resume drinking.

Pearlman entered the Topic. He was short, squat, mousy. He seemed lonely and ill at ease. Stratton pointed him out to Candace, explaining about the Independence option which had three weeks to run. Suddenly Stratton said, "Would you dance with that fellow for $2,500?" Candace looked blank. Stratton said, "I mean for three weeks. Could you keep Mr. Pearlman very busy for three weeks?" The girl smiled. For an instant she didn't look a bit confused. She nodded briskly. Stratton went down to Pearlman. He led him back to the gallery. Candace reached shyly for Pearlman's arm and drew him down beside her. Pearlman glowed. Plainly he wasn't used to being fussed over by women as pretty as Candace. Stratton left them a little later. Pearlman was ordering champagne and lobster. Candace was planted charmingly on his lap.

But even with Candace on the job and with John Harnan at the Independence, Stratton slept badly for three weeks. He had a recurrent nightmare. In it Pearlman entered the abandoned crosscut with Candace and the Topic dance band and a waiter carrying champagne and lobster. Pearlman probed the wall with his lobster fork—and found the vein. On the night before the option was to expire, Stratton had dinner at the Palace Hotel with Pearlman and Candace. Afterward they sat in the lobby before the great fireplace where spruce logs burned on summer evenings. Pearlman complained that the Independence hadn't shown much stuff. He had barely made expenses. He said, "See here, Stratton, you might as well take back your option tonight. I don't want it. Candace and I are leaving for 'Frisco in the morning."

Pearlman held out the option. Stratton trembled so that he was afraid to reach for it. Not Candace. She grabbed it and tossed it in the fire. Pearlman stepped to the cigar counter a moment. Stratton slipped Candace five $500 bills. In a practiced maneuver, Candace raised her petticoat. The bills vanished in the top of her black stocking. She murmured to Stratton. "Won't be gone long. I just want to see the Golden Gate."

There was a large celebration in Stratton's cabin that night. His guests were Jimmy Burns, Jimmy Doyle and John Harnan. The way was clear now. They could proceed with the Portland-Independence plot. Next day Stratton blocked out work along the Independence vein and hired a large crew. He designed his surface structures and hired contractors to build them. He signed freighting agreements for ore shipments to Pueblo. According to his schedule the mine would be shipping 30 tons a day by September. He restricted his net profit to $60,000 a month, for he believed that gold in the ground was worth more than gold in circulation.

Meanwhile Burns put 100 men to digging in the Portland on three 8-hour shifts. Some secrecy was still maintained. The high-grade was hauled at night, but not on the backs of two Irishmen. A dozen ore wagons were used instead. Of course the gold camp was aware that something was happening at the Portland. Burns planted the rumor that Dave Moffat, the Denver banker, was financing it. And a full month passed before word got out that the richness of the mine itself permitted the financing. The surrounding claim owners dilly-dallied. They didn't get their apex suits into court until mid-November. By then Burns had a defense fund of $125,000. Stratton had $180,000 earned from the Independence. And he had established unlimited bank credit.

Twenty-seven Battle Mountain owners filed suits, claiming prior rights to the Portland vein. The suits asked total damages of $3,000,000. Stratton was ready for them. He felt that he had found a man with the imagination, the gall and the energy to rout the Portland's enemies. He had known Verner Z. Reed for years in Colorado Springs and had marveled at this brilliant mind. This Reed, just turned 30, had sold ten times as many lots and homes as any other real estate agent by an invention which he called "the installment plan." Reed was a F. Scott Fitzgerald character twenty-five years ahead of the Jazz Age. He had a Fitzgeraldian beauty, a love of gilded living and an ability to earn vast sums of money with great ease. He had started out as a *Chicago Tribune* reporter and had moved to Little London in the late 80's. Soon he was famous as a press agent and as author of some of the warmest novels ever to shock and delight Victorian prudery. Stratton read Reed's third book, *Tales of the Sun-Land,* and burned it in horror. The book described amorous activities seldom discussed even at Hazel Vernon's. It contained illustrations of males and maidens together, obviously unclothed.

Stratton brought Reed to Cripple and installed him in the bridal suite at the Palace. Reed tore into the Portland mess with such fury that the twenty-seven suers were unable to catch up with him. He exploited the law of apex in reverse by purchasing fringe claims and informing the suers that *their* veins probably apexed on the fringe claims. So why were they suing the Portland? The Portland actually should be suing them.

Then he optioned the Portland claim to a dummy firm for $250,000. The twenty-seven suers began to get frightened. They were not sure whom to sue now. Finally they sued the dummy firm. Reed dissolved it. The option reverted to the Burns, Doyle and Harnan partnership. The suers resumed suing the Irishmen. Next day Reed dissolved the partnership. The Portland claim, he said, was owned actually by something called the Portland Gold Mining Company. Stratton gave Reed $90,000 and Reed declared a big Portland dividend. Portland stock rocketed on the world's mining exchanges. The Portland Gold Mining Company became overnight one of Colorado's most valuable enterprises.

Bewildered and panicky, the Portland's foes called Reed into conference. When it ended, they had sold to him all claims involved in the twenty-seven lawsuits. Jimmy Doyle's house-lot patch expanded to 183 acres, comprising a third of the mountain. Reed paid for these claims $1,025,000, much of it borrowed by Stratton. Reed issued 3 million shares of Portland stock. Stratton took 731,000 shares. Burns, Doyle and Harnan received 600,000 shares each. Stratton didn't attend the first stockholders' meeting and he was elected president of the Portland company. He resigned, stating that it was up to the Irishmen to run it. Harum-scarum Doyle was not interested. Neither was Harnan, who was a heavy gambler and boozer. Jimmy Burns became president by default.

While Reed was handling the Portland fight, Stratton strengthened the position of his Independence by purchasing eleven adjoining claims. That gave him 112 acres. Sam Strong wouldn't sell his Strong Mine just below the Independence. But northward up the mountain Stratton's territory abutted the new Portland territory. It totaled 112 acres. As Stratton had predicted, he and the Irishmen virtually owned Battle Mountain. Stratton, of course, had much the largest holdings of the four.

It was late December now in '93. Cripple had many fine producing mines but none to compare with the Portland and Independence. Stratton had read a lot of gold history. He realized that he had on his hands two properties which might be richer than India's

Kolar, Brazil's Morroe Velho, Columbia's Antioquia, Australia's Bendige, Nevada's Comstock. Winfield Stratton, a carpenter by trade, was on his way to becoming wealthier and more powerful than the kings of Europe, the rail barons of America, the war lords of China. As he thought it over he decided the time had come for extravagance. He wrote Bert Robbins' store in Little London asking Bert to send him a new pair of shoes and a light felt hat.

He needed the shoes and hat very soon. Candace Root had come to call, driving a gig purchased, she said, out of $2,500 which she had earned recently. She brought an invitation. Could Stratton attend Christmas dinner at the Myers Avenue residence of Miss Hazel Vernon? Punch would be served a 1 o'clock. Guests would sit down to the turkey an hour later. Stratton despised ordinary social functions. But Hazel Vernon's dinners were far from ordinary. And it was a rare distinction to be the guest of Cripple's most distinguished madame.

Stratton told Candace he would be there.

Christmas Day was warm and sunny, almost

like summer. There was no snow. Stratton donned his stiff shirt, high collar, black velvet tie and black alpaca suit. He put on his new shoes and his new hat. Jimmy Burns picked him up in his shiny red buggy. Burns would escort Georgia Hayden to Hazel's dinner. He wore a suit of the very latest cut and a fashionable gray derby. Jimmy seemed to Stratton to have just stepped off Fifth Avenue.

It was a nice ride to town. Stratton, normally solemn, felt festive as the smart buggy drew up to the familiar Myers Avenue stoop. Hazel's girls had garlanded the entrance in spruce bows held up with red ribbons. The first-floor windows, usually curtained, were gay with Christmas trees. In the small lobby, where customers deposited their wallets, Stratton greeted the colored butler, who was dressed like Santa Claus. Hazel had made the reception room into a banquet hall. The straight chairs where the girls sat for selection were gone. In their place was a rose punch bowl with candles behind accentuating the sparkle of the champagne. The banquet table was covered with white damask. The table was set for thirty people. The service was solid silver and the dishes equal in quality to those Stratton had seen in General Palmer's Glen Eyrie castle. He doubted, though, if the General boasted place-card holders like Hazel's. They were tiny nude maidens with exuberant breasts which propped up the place cards.

A three-piece band played Strauss waltzes in a corner of the room. Hazel Vernon, statuesque and authoritative in a dress of red beads, stood by the band, welcoming her guests. Her nine girls were lined up beyond, demure in their best gowns. Stratton felt peaceful and at home. He knew this world. There was Sam Strong, expensively clothed now but otherwise the same burly boor who had barged in on Stratton's hill in '91. Sam had made enough money to burn a wet dog with. The tall, thin girl on his arm was his mistress, Nellie Lewis. Stratton bowed to Grant Crumley, the handsomest man in Cripple. Grant had been with the Dalton gang until the Daltons were wiped out in Coffeyville, Kansas. He had escaped and had come to Colorado with Grace Carlyle, the lovely blonde at his side now. Grace had sung in a Coffeyville church choir. The choirmaster seduced her in a back pew one night and his wife caught him. That is why Grace left Coffeyville with Grant. Her angel's face was a trifle deceptive. She loved to climb on bars and remove her clothes while the customer chanted "Down goes McGinty!" She was whimsical. Once she tried to shoot a doctor who had saved her life by pumping laudanum [a form of opium] from her stomach.

Georgia Hayden looked luscious as a ripe peach beside the shining Burns. She was turning her charm on a sharp-faced lad in his early twenties, Charlie MacNeill, a milling genius who had built the world's first chlorination plant on Wilson Creek below Stratton's cabin. Charlie was accompanied by a spectacular, big-bosomed, big-hipped girl almost 6 feet tall, named Sally Halthusen, a daughter of a Springs sheep-and-grain man. Sally had the outside structure of a Gibson girl. But inside she was packed with fierce desire instead of sweet gentility. She was said to have collected $10,000 from a Denver father to remove her outside structure from the vicinity of his son. Sally liked men as big and husky as herself and she always had a lot of big fellows around. But what she liked most was horses. She could mount the wildest bronc in Colorado and tame him. One of Cripple's finest sights was Sally astride her white thoroughbred moving along Bennett Avenue. Sally, like Georgia Hayden, was on the prowl for a rich man. But, whereas Georgia wanted luxury and social position, Sally just wanted to get going on a horse farm.

A fter four glasses of champagne punch, Stratton was as gay as a lamb. He was touched to find that Hazel had placed him at the head of the table. He carved the turkeys with a skill derived from his carpentry work. Hazel's maids served red Burgundy and a sweet wine with dessert and more champagne with the coffee and brandy. The band played Christmas carols and everyone sang. Hiram Rogers, the *Gazette* reporter, organized some charades. Whisky bottles began to appear on the table. Toward 6 o'clock the songs became quite bawdy. So did the charades. And the room lost its unnatural decorum. Hazel withdrew to rest before the evening's business was started. Two of her girls were smoking cigars. One was dancing on the table. Another was trying to stand on her head. Sally Halthusen was tickling Hiram Rogers. Jimmy Burns, drunk now but still dapper, was scowling at Charlie MacNeill who was showing Georgia Hayden a wrestling hold. Hiram Rogers came over to Stratton and asked him casually how much he was worth now. Stratton considered a moment. "Maybe a million, Hiram," he said. "Not much more." Shortly after, Stratton shook hands all around and left Hazel Vernon's. He was glad to ride alone in a rented hack back to his own quiet cabin. He was oversated with food and drink and the smell of perfume and strong cigars.

But Stratton had had one of the best Christmases of his whole life.

He was in the Palace Hotel lobby next day when the stage arrived. He heard newsboys hawking the Colorado Springs Gazette. One entered the lobby shouting, "Cripple's first millionaire!" Stratton scratched his chin and wondered who the millionaire could be. The newsboy pushed a *Gazette* before him. Across the front page were the letters: "WINFIELD SCOTT STRATTON." Hiram Rogers' subhead read: "Well-known Carpenter Counts His Worth in Seven Figures."

That story was picked up by hundreds of papers. It marked the start of a Cripple Creek boom that would last nine years and would create fifty more millionaires. A thousand others would pile up fortunes of $50,000 or more. Gold production would reach $20,000,000 annually, making Cripple the richest gold camp on earth. The population would touch 50,000. The limits of Cripple Creek town would push up Mount Pisgah's slopes until they encompassed an area of 640 acres. The camp would have 150 saloons, seventy-five of which would be on or near the swaybacked length of Bennett Avenue. The monthly payroll of miners would be a million dollars. The Colorado Springs Mining Exchange would list the stocks of 450 Cripple Creek companies. Gambling on these stocks would be a favorite pastime at every crossroads community. Celebrated geologists and milling men and financiers and lawyers would rush to Pikes Peak. School children in Maine and Texas would sing the jingle:

Goin' up to Cripple Creek,
Goin' on the run,
Goin' up to Cripple Creek,
To have a little fun!

At the center of the excitement was the tall, thin, pale carpenter. Winfield Stratton's income from '94 on was a million dollars a year from the Independence alone. Still more gold came from his Portland holdings. The Portland, however, wasn't anywhere near as rich as the Independence which was netting 64 cents for every dollar's worth of ore mined. Some Independence ore realized $4 a pound. Portland ore seldom brought more than $4 a ton.

Jimmy Burns had developed into a superb mine manager. The ability he had used to plan good bathrooms helped him to direct a Portland crew of 500 miners, the largest in Colorado. He installed the most advanced machinery, the speediest steam hoists, rapid new multiple drills, the safest in underground trams. Jimmy Doyle and John Harnan were both Portland executives, too, but it was Burns' creative drive that made things go.

Stratton had known for years that Burns was gifted and ambitious. And yet he was unprepared for the great administrative skill which Burns displayed. Burns had been born in Portland, Maine, in 1850. His father was Scotch, his mother Irish. In his twenties he became head of the family which included three adoring spinster sisters and a younger brother. He also supported an orphan child, Jimmy Doyle, whom his sisters had taken in with the same compassion they had for stray cats. Jimmy Doyle loved the sisters dearly and earned his keep by doing chores for them. When the Burns family came to Colorado Springs in 1886, Doyle came, too, and worked as delivery boy for the sisters in their seamstress business.

For some years prior to his Springs arrival,

Jimmy Burns had had a roving career running sugar machinery on plantations in Cuba and in South America. Once on a Cuban plantation he fell into a pit which had been dug to catch wild animals. This pit had caught a boa constrictor instead. The boa had been down there some time and was ravenously hungry. While Jimmy's helpers rushed for ropes to pull him from the deep pit, the boa moved slowly toward him. In those seconds, Jimmy's hair turned a dazzling white and white it remained. Or so Jimmy used to say.

His first job in Little London was driving a road grader. Then he took up plumbing and steam fitting. He was a hot-tempered, positive little man in perpetual revolt against the status quo. He was raised a good Catholic but he sometimes horrified his devout sisters by asking pointed questions about parts of the Catholic doctrine. He was a born social climber. His upward climb in Little London society began in '88 when he was elected foreman of the Hook and Ladder Fire Company No. 1.

In 1890 he asked the city fathers to name him

sewer inspector. They turned him down but he got sweet revenge by forcing the city council to pay him $10 damages for the loss of a $5 pair of pants which were burned while Jimmy was on fire duty.

One of Stratton's pleasures was watching the ease with which Mr. James Ferguson Burns, president of the Portland Gold Mining Company, slipped into the glittering world of his dreams. Stratton recalled how haughty members of the Springs banking fraternity used to order Burns to unclog a toilet which flooded one their North End mansions. Now these same financiers jolted their bones springing to attention whenever the ex-plumber entered their banks. Burns planned to buy a North End mansion himself. Stratton was a little sad about Georgia Hayden. When she learned about Jimmy's wealth, she offered him her soul and body forever. Jimmy was pleased but set no wedding date. As months passed, Georgia grew frightened. She borrowed $1,000 from Stratton to defray the cost of redesigning her wardrobe and her figure along lines which would charm Jimmy. He was not charmed. At last he told her she was a sweet girl but her curves no longer blinded him to the fact that she was not suitable for the social circles he planned to enter.

Once a month Jimmy visited Denver's best tailor to be fitted for four new suits. He held frequent press conferences at Johnny Nolon's where reporters and engineers hung pop-eyed on his words. He rented by the year the right-hand box at the Butte Opera House. He always got the best table at Topic variety shows. Burns had a real love of any kind of theater. He would express this love one day by building in Colorado Springs a theater which is still one of the handsomest structures in Colorado.

But Jimmy Burns, compared to Winfield Stratton, was a small splash. Stratton was the great surge, the stirring note that thrilled gold campers by day and lulled them to sleep at night. Horace Tabor, the Leadville grocer whose silver profits astounded the world in the 80's, had amassed a mere $8,000,000. Dave Moffat, the mighty promoter, wasn't worth that much. Tom Walsh hadn't begun to get from his Camp Bird Mine at Ouray the eventual $6,000,000 which would help him buy the Hope diamond for his daughter.

But Stratton! He had $10,000,000 already! He knew, of course, how tremendously he impressed people. And yet he refused to be impressed by himself. His Independence Mine was known around the world. Great geologists talked of it to him, their voices shaking with emotion. Stratton treated it with no more concern than he would have treated any carpentry job to be worked according to estimate. There were no college-trained experts on his payroll. Old friends like Charlie Steele and Fred Trautman ran the mine. Stratton's general manager was his shoe-maker, a Swiss named Bob Schwarz. Stratton did not change his habits. Through '94 and most of '95 he lived alone in the Wilson Creek cabin, on one side of which he added a porch at a cost of $87.16. He did hire a cook and a night watchman. The watchman's duties were mostly confined to distributing $5 bills to Myers Avenue women who called to see if Stratton were lonely. Many Battle Mountain supers took in these perambulating prostitutes as regularly as the morning milk. Stratton had no desire. His mine absorbed him.

As early as '94, Stratton started philanthropies the results of which are visible today throughout the Pikes Peak region. He gave $85,000 to the Salvation Army, $20,000 to Colorado College, $25,000 to the Colorado School of Mines. He gave thousands to Cripple Creek churches. When Horace Tabor hit the skids, Stratton loaned him $15,000 and tore up the note. He reimbursed dozens of poor widows and nursemaids who had lost money on a gyp promotion of one of his early claims. Any old miner down on his luck could drop in at Stratton's cabin and get $100. Stratton supplied all poor families in the Battle Mountain area with free coal. When his presumed son by Zeurah Stewart turned up, Stratton made arrangements to pay him $100 a month for life and enrolled him at the University of Illinois. He donated a bicycle to every laundry girl in Colorado Springs. During a blizzard, he paid men to feed the horned larks.

BOOM TIMES
IN CRIPPLE CREEK

"THE WORLD'S RICHEST GOLD FIELDS"
& COLORADO SPRINGS "THE HOME OF MINING
KINGS" 1890–1900

"GOLD IS WHERE YOU FIND IT..."

Left: *Winfield Scott Stratton. Stratton became Cripple Creek's first millionaire and one of the region's most generous benefactors when the Independence Mine began production in 1893. The story of the mine's discovery relates that on the night of July 3, 1891 Stratton dreamed that a brier–covered dyke he had by-passed earlier was a gold mine. The following morning, July 4, he returned to Cripple Creek, found the spot he had seen in his dream, and staked the Washington and Independence claims. Portrait from: Representative Men of Colorado, in the Nineteenth Century. Rowell Art Publishing, 190*
Right: *James Ferguson Burns. Obituary, Gazette Telegraph Newspaper, September 24, 1917.*

The Independence, Winfield Scott Stratton's "dream mine," yielded $2,272,000 in dividends by 1900. Stratton sold the mine in 1899 to an English syndicate for $11 million through his agent, Verner Z. Re The white frame house in the foreground is where Stratton lived during his years in Cripple Creek whil he developed the Independence and other interests. Independence Mine c. 1896. Photographer Unknow

Pikes Peak from Cripple Creek. In 1890 the name of Cripple Creek was only used to describe the area around Florissant by homesteaders and ranchers and by pioneer, Bob Womack, wandering cowboy and perpetual prospector. In April, 1891, the name became official as claim holders established boundaries for the new District: Rholite Mountain on the North; Big Bull Hill on the East; Steaub Mountain on the South; Mount Pisgah on the West. Between 1893 and 1900 mines multiplied and the District changed into a modern industrial center. The District's population soared to 55,000 boasting 500 mines with an annual production of over $18 million, 73 saloons, eight newspapers, three banks, 16 churches, a stock exchange, schools, street cars, and a thriving commercial District by the turn-of-the-century. Pikes Peak from the Buena Vista, Cripple Creek c. 1893 Photographer: William Hook.

Robert Womack. "The Father of Cripple Creek" found gold but never struck it rich. Womack's family settled in the area near Florissant on property homesteaded by Levi Welty. Discredited by the Mt. Pisgah Hoax of 1884, Womack became a local character telling anyone who would listen about the gold ore waiting to be claimed, including an unconvinced W. S. Stratton. For many years, Poverty Gulch seemed a good name for the area he prospected until the El Paso Lode, he located in 1890 with a gold content assaying at $250 a ton. This ignited the run for Cripple Creek and the discovery in rapid succession of some of the richest gold deposits in the world. Womack sold his discovery for $500 believing another claim could be his bonanza. Womack never became one of Cripple Creek's famous millionaires. Helped financially by Stratton and others in later years, he was almost forgotten until 1902 when the town of Cripple Creek turned out to honor him for his discovery. Bob Womack died in 1902. Portrait by Unknown Photographer. The C.O.D. Mine located in the misnamed Poverty Gulch, was owned by Charles L. Tutt and the Spencer Penrose. Man standing by white horse is believed to be Spencer Penrose. C.O.D. Mine, July 22, 1893. Photographer: Unknown.

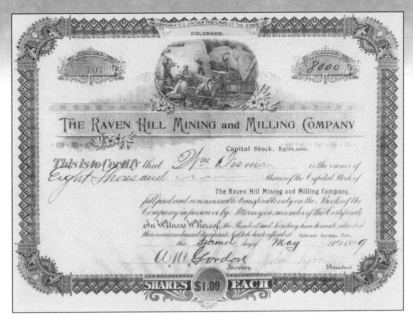

Stock Certificate for the Raven Hill Mining and Milling Company, May 2, 1899. Donated by : John Hann

Raven Hill. Situated on the southern slope of Raven Hill. The property was located by E. M. De La Vergne, M. F. Stark, E. R. Stark and Thomas Stark. Photographer: William Hook c. 1893.

First Assay Office in Cripple Creek. A. L. Dana, assayer stands near the door. Assayers could be scientists, alchemists, psychologists and promoters for mining districts. First Assay Office, c. 1893. Gift of C. N. Freeman.

Miners at the Strong Mine located by Sam Strong who played a colorful role in the District's history. Young boys with dogs seem ready to take their place with the men who worked the mines.

Visitors arrive by stage at the Palace Hotel (Northwest corner of 2nd and Bennett). Until the arrival of railroads to the District in 1894, stagelines provided transportation from the terminals in Florence and Divide. The Hundley Stage Coach Service ran five coaches daily every day of the week. The Palace served as hotel, meeting place, mining exchange and chamber of commerce. Palace Hotel c. 1893. Photographer: Unknown.

Pikes Peak from Colorado Springs. Pikes Peak Avenue c. 1890. In 1890 Colorado Springs retained the genteel aura of Little London offering "hope and scenery" to tourists and healthseekers. Discovery of gold in Cripple Creek brought dramatic changes: The population tripled from 11,000 to 30,000 while bank deposits increased nine times as Cripple Creek mines paid unprecedented dividends. Here General Palmer's first Antlers Hotel (1880-1898) serenely awaits guests and the future. "Pikes Peak at Himself" c. 1889 Photographers: Rudy and Clinton.

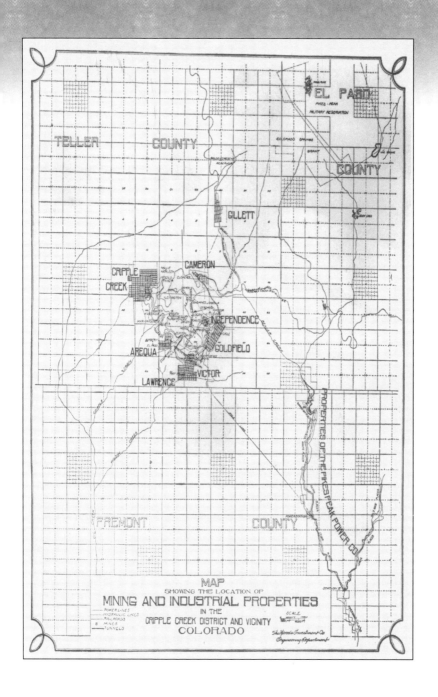

Map showing "Location of Mining and Industrial Properties in the Cripple Creek District." Promotional brochure of Cripple Creek by Woods Investment Co., c. 1900.

Crapper Jack's Dance Hall where some of the action in the King of Cripple Creek takes place claimed high honors as one of the liveliest dance halls in the Red Light District. Popular girls pictured here are said to include: Dirty Neck Nell;, Dizzy Daisy, Tall Rose, Bilious Bessie, Slippery Sadie, Greasy Greta, and Victor Pig.

Cripple Creek's first newspaper The Weekly Crusher began publication on December 10, 189. Offices for the newspaper were in this log cabin.

In the early days a square meal cost only 25 cents at the Miner's Home tent. The Palace Hotel offered more elaborate fare proclaiming the best the market affords in "fish, flesh, fowl and other delicate luxuries."

Death in Saloon. Life could be short and end violently in the boom days of the District. Sam Strong, early Battle Mountain prospector and mine owner, fell victim to three weaknesses of the mining camps--women, whiskey and gambling. Tried and acquitted of bombing the Strong Mine in the strike of 1894, the nineties for Sam were marked by a series of fights and lawsuits that ended only when he was shot by saloon-owner, Grant Crumley. This photo, of doubtful authenticity, records the scene of the shooting and its aftermath. Photographer: Unknown, 1902.

Card players wear congenial smiles as they count their chips during an evening's entertainment.

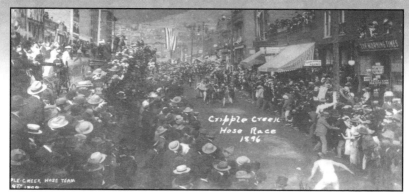

The Cripple Creek Hose Race of 1899 took place along a street of brick-line buildings.

First fire barely contained by using dynamite when second fire started on Wednesday and finished the destruction on the town built on gold but made of wood. Desolation on Myers Avenue. Photographer: Unknown.

On Saturday, April 25, 1896 a fire started at the Central Dance Hall when dance hall girl toppled gasoline stove in a fight. Blurred figures and galloping horses attempt to escape the chaos of fire. Photographer: Unknown.

Tripple Creek Rebuilt in Stone before the year ended. William and Welty Livery Stable was ready for business in new building in the 200 block of Bennett Avenue. Photographer: Courtesy of Al Welty.

Festooned carriage for one of many Cripple Creek celebrations. Bennett Avenue c. 1898. Photograph: Courtesy of Al Welty.

Cripple Creek Builds to last... Intricate and elaborate facades of the Weinberger and Aspen Builds reflect confidence and optimism of the business community in 1896. Weinberger Building. Photographer: Norm Sams.

ke-Driving Competitions tested skills of miners. Young boy holds stop watch timing contestants in urth of July Competition of 1897.

e Colorado Springs Mining Exchange where some of the members paused for a photograph. The nouncement on board notifies members about the banquet honoring W.S. Stratton who built the hange. Everyone who was anyone and invited attended the banquet on January 16, 1902-- everyone t Winfield Scott Stratton. Colorado Springs Mining Exchange January 16, 1902. Photographer: warts Brothers.

Pikes Peak Avenue in Colorado Springs in 1903 reflects the change of the decade including the second Antlers Hotel, the Mining Exchange building, the Independence Building, and tracks for Stratton's new streetcar system. The statue in background of Zebulon Pike marks the 125th anniversary of exploration. Pikes Peak Avenue, c. 1903. Photographer: Unknown.

Stratton Park where new streetcars carried townspeople for recreation and amusements. In 1900 Stratton purchased 20 acres of the Dixon Ranch near Cheyenne Canyon for $40,000 and donated the area to the residents of Colorado Springs. Residents enjoyed the park for many years. Like Streetcar #52, Stratton streetcars were luxurious cars that moved throughout the city.

Left: *The bandstand was a popular destination on Sunday afternoons.*
Right: *Playground–Stratton Park. "The Rocker." Park Photographs: Harry Standley*

eft: Stratton Building, Colorado Springs: c. 1905. Photographer: Unknown.

ight: New Post Office Building marked transition and growth of Colorado Springs.

The Myron Stratton Home dedicated to the memory of Winfield Scott Stratton's father provided homes and assistance for El Paso County residents. Myron Stratton Home, c. 1942.

Winfield Scott Stratton Memorial by Nellie V. Walker, Myron Stratton Home. Photographer: Unknown.

"Weeping Angels" Monument at Stratton Grave in Evergreen Cemetery. Sculpted by Nellie V. Walker. Inscription reads: "It is not enough to support the feeble up/ But to support him after." Save Outdoor Sculpture Collection.

His deepest interest, however, was in helping Cripple Creek to grow. Cheap transportation was essential as mining costs increased with depth. The vertical climb for supplies coming to camp from the plains at the Springs was 4,000 feet. From the plains at Canon City the climb was 4,700 feet. In either case the road distance was 45 miles. Stratton and Burns convinced financiers that the production of the Independence and the Portland by themselves justified heavy investment in transportation. Two spectacular railroads reached the district. The three stage roads were improved. Somewhat later a network of picturesque electric cars served the whole 10,000-acre area.

Stratton was determined to keep the district a true gold camp where any poor man could try his luck because the ground had not been gobbled up by huge companies. Such camps benefited many people instead of a few absentee owners, wildcat promoters, stockbrokers and lawyers. Stratton did not wait long to show how he felt about absentee owners. In '94, twelve of them from Little London tried to increase Cripple's work day from eight to nine hours. The day's pay remained at $3. The absentee owners argued that hard times prevailed elsewhere. Therefore Cripple's miners should be glad to take what amounted to a wage cut even though Cripple Creek itself was prospering.

The 1,200 miners were rugged individualists. They were woodsmen, hunters, anglers and foragers. Their answer to the mine owners was to join the new Western Federation of Miners. Their leader, a quiet Scot named John Calderwood, told them to stop work and seize most of Bull Hill and Battle Mountain. He created a principality. Anyone wishing to enter it from the United States had to have a passport and visa. The Independence and Portland were situated within Calderhood's principality. The absentee owners came to Stratton and Burns and pledged their cooperation in all moves the titans made to recover their property from the anarchists. Stratton sent the owners down the mountain rejoicing. He assured them that he and Burns would act decisively. The owners assumed that at the very least he would ask

President Cleveland for a regiment of regulars to come up from Fort Logan to capture Bull Hill.

Stratton and Burns did act.

Burns flatly refused to raise the Portland work day to nine hours. He issued a statement praising his employees for joining the Western Federation of Miners. "Every worker," Jimmy added, "has a right to improve his status by bargaining collectively." In its report, The *Cripple Creek Crusher* commented: "Upon receipt of Mr. Burns' statement, three mine owners at the El Paso Club collapsed on the pool table and died of apoplexy."

Stratton's action was worse. He asked the miner's leader, John Calderwood, to his cabin to discuss a compromise. Calderwood came, accepted Stratton's proposal and a contract was signed. A contract with the Western Federation of Miners! To the absentee owners, Burns' approval of collective bargaining was heresy. But Stratton's act in signing a contract with the foe was rank treason. It was blasphemous for him even to admit that Calderwood and the Western Federation existed.

The bitter, bloody strike continued for four months, one of the first great strikes in modern labor history. The miners won. They credited their victory to the help they received at the start from Stratton and Burns and to the intervention of Populist Governor Davis H. Waite, for whom Stratton and Burns had voted in '92.

G old campers were grateful another time to the carpenter and the plumber. On a blowy April day in '96, a bartender beat up his mistress in their room above the Central Dance Hall. He knocked over the gasoline stove. The wind fanned the flames and the business section of Cripple Creek town was destroyed in two hours. Four days later a second fire started, this time in the Portland Hotel kitchen. The wind was blowing much harder. Hysteria set in. The terror reached a peak when the Palace Hotel boilers exploded and 700 pounds of dynamite went off in a grocery store. The streets, full of suffocating smoke and bits of flying fire, were nightmarish with runaway horses trampling women and children and frenzied saloon men trying to roll away whisky barrels. Parlor-house girls in nightgowns and customers wearing less screamed at upstairs windows. Some girls had pets in their arms and pleaded to passers-by to save the pets at least.

The wind ceased at nightfall. Then it was easy to control the fire. But the weather turned cold as the sun sank behind Mount Pisgah. Five thousand people were without shelter away up there on top of the world. All food, covering, cooking utensils and fuel had been consumed. Men began looting to feed their families. But this trend was averted by one bright factor. Word got around that Stratton and Burns were organizing a shipment of relief supplies from Little London.

This second fire had been burning only an hour when Burns got through to the Springs on Cripple's one telephone. At the Springs end were Stratton, Verner Reed and others. When Burns finished his report Stratton said, "Gentlemen, we can see that a catastrophe has come. We must move. We have no time for money pledges. Charge everything to me."

In thirty minutes Stratton had formed the Springs' citizenry into relief committees. He drove to the Colorado Midland depot and ordered a special train. Twelve freight wagons were rushed to the wholesale grocery where volunteers loaded twenty-five cases of canned beef, six cases of beans, six cases of condensed milk, twelve crates of crackers and a thousand loaves of bread—in all $50,000 worth of items were charged to Stratton. He called the department stores and cornered their blanket supply, sending 500 pairs to the rail depot. Also 750 diapers. A committee collected 165 eight-person tents and a tabernacle tent.

Before dark the supplies were loaded into two box cars. The special train rattled up Ute Pass at 15 miles an hour, which was very fast for that 4 percent grade. Meanwhile Cripple's residents had formed their own relief committees. Most of the 5,000 homeless gathered at the reservoir above the charred, smoldering town. Georgia Hayden and Sally Halthusen put some sporting women to running a nursery corral where tired mothers could park their children. The mothers had no qualms. During many pneumonia epidemics Myers Avenue girls had proved to be excellent nurses.

At 9 p.m. the reservoir crowd whooped and whistled when the headlights of the relief train appeared around Gold Hill. As the special raced down the slope and across Poverty Gulch it looked like the Fourth of July. The firebox poured out streams of white-hot coals. Every drive wheel was a circle of sparks from the grinding brakeshoes. The engineer blew his whistle most of the way to the depot at the east end of Bennett. A hundred men with oil torches met the train. Two dozen four-horse freight wagons waited in a line stretching off from the platform. All night the teams hauled supplies up the hill for distribution. Meanwhile Stratton sent a second relief train roaring up Ute Pass. In the morning, classes at Colorado College were canceled and the students combed the North End for jam, vegetables, fruit, boiled eggs, hams, clothes, dishes, firewood. They brought their loot to a central point where Stratton posted several transfer wagons.

Because of the old man's rapid action the gold campers were comfortable long before the fire was entirely out in the ruined town. Some 3,000 people found lodging by doubling up with friends throughout the district. Two thousand more were under tents. Within two days Catholic and Congregational services were held in the scorched depot. Ella Holden resumed trade at her parlor house, The Library. Pearl Sevan raised a tin structure to replace her Sunnyrest. The piano player at Casey's saloon was beating out *Do You Like Tutti-Frutti?* even as the carpenters banged away at the corrugated iron enclosing the new establishment. School children went to classes in the basement of the Sisters of Mercy Hospital. A tarpaper restaurant in the middle of the debris of Bennett Avenue advertised joyfully: "Strawberries and Pure Cream, 15 cents."

The burning of Cripple Creek turned out to be a blessing. The hundreds of shacks, built hastily of poor lumber in '92 and '93, were about to fall down anyhow. They were uncomfortable, unsanitary eyesores. The fire destroyed immense accumulations of trash and garbage. It destroyed privies far beyond the redemption stage.

The rapid reconstruction and transformation of the town during the summer of '96 was like a miracle. Handsome redbrick buildings with tasteful cupolas and a variety of gables replaced the ugly barns that had formed the business district. The new frame residences were of excellent architectural design—the best Victorian gingerbread. Cripple didn't look like a transient mining community any more. It had an air of pride and stability.

Nobody dreamed that the stability would be brief, lasting only as long as the life of its most prominent citizen. People were too busy making money to look ahead. They had time, however, to marvel at the continuing exploits of Winfield Stratton. It was not merely that the stooped old man was ten times richer than any other gold camp millionaire. What amazed everyone was his attitude toward money. It didn't mean a thing to him. As his molehill of gold grew into a mountain, the world crowded around to watch him do the expected. He would buy a United States senatorship as Horace Tabor had done. Or he might buy a countess in Paris and cover her in underwear of pure gold. He would buy Russian pearls and Arabian horses and Italian paintings. His great yacht would commute between his Venetian palazzo and his rambling summer place at Newport. For a home he would buy a frosty palace a Versailles.

Stratton didn't buy a palace at Versailles. Late in '95, when he left his Wilson Creek cabin and moved to the Springs, he even refused to buy a mansion in the North End. Verner Reed and Jimmy Burns bought homes on North Tejon Street. Burns planned a much bigger home on that coming millionaires row, Wood Avenue. Sam Altman, who had paid Blanche Barton long ago, bought the aristocratic Cascade Avenue residence of Count James Pourtales.

And Stratton? He bought an unimposing $5,000 clapboard house downtown which he himself had built years earlier for a client. His return to Little

London created a problem among the feminine arbiters of North End society. They had been sorry when he had gone to Cripple in '91. They had known him as that clever carpenter who had been so good and so discreet about making any little thing they wanted—a form on which to hang their corsets or a secret cupboard for their padded matildas or a lock on their bedroom door strong enough to bar a husband who had drunk too much at the El Paso Club.

Now Stratton was back. But not as a carpenter. Instead he was one of the most important men on earth. What should their attitude toward him be? All his millions, of course, could not buy for him a place in their charmed circle, much as he must yearn for that place. Heaven forbid! And yet Stratton's wealth was so staggering that perhaps it was not quite the same thing as mere vulgar money. Perhaps it was more like a divine dispensation. It might not be gauche therefore to permit him to place his foot in their social door.

Or so it seemed to some of the North End ladies. Others said no. As far as they were concerned,

Mr. Stratton remained a crude carpenter just as Jimmy Burns remained a profane plumber and Sam Strong a boorish roustabout. "We will not compromise our standards! Breeding tells, my dear." For months the dear ladies argued. A few called at Stratton's modest home. They found him polite but— and this perplexed them—reluctant to allow them beyond the front hall. A few asked him to tea. He did not appear. A few condescended to speak to him on the streets. He acknowledged their greetings with grave courtesy. But the puzzlement in his pale blue eyes told them that he didn't have the slightest notion who they were. One brave soul threw caution to the winds. She invited Mr. Stratton to the most elaborate dinner party that it was possible to arrange. She wrote for oysters to be shipped from New Orleans, a ham from Richmond and a fine white wine from Lake Erie as a super grace note. The invitations went out, engraved in letters high enough to cut a millionaire dowager's finger.

The acceptances poured in.

From Stratton she received a note of regret.

Not from Stratton himself, but from his secretary, William Ramsay. And so a last the truth dawned on the bewildered ladies. Stratton didn't give a damn for the whole kit and kaboodle of them!

It was inevitable that Stratton should be drawn into politics during one of the bitterest of presidential campaigns, the McKinley-Bryan struggle of '96. Four years earlier he had supported free silver, Senator Teller and the Populists. Grover Cleveland and the gold bugs had won. The Silver Purchase Act was repealed, the price of silver collapsed and the country was saved for Wall Street and the gold standard. Of course it was slightly embarrassing to the enriched gold bugs to have the Panic of '93 instead of the prosperity they had promised.

Meanwhile Stratton had inherited a mountain of gold. If ever there was a king of the gold bugs he was that king. He must realize how foolish he had been to back silver against his own interest. Surely he would denounce William Jennings Bryan now. He would line up behind gold, William McKinley and Senator Ed Wolcott.

And Ed Wolcott thought, one fall week end while watching the swans at his Wolhurst estate, how splendid it would be to have Stratton as chief benefactor of the Republican Party! In October of '96 Wolcott sent his Springs agent to Stratton for a campaign contribution. Not a sensational amount to start. Say $100,000. Stratton listened closely. He nodded with vigor as the agent explained that McKinley's election meant a continued high gold price and continued low wages. Gold, the agent said, was top dog and must remain so. He concluded with a hint that the Republican Party would be honored to receive Stratton's financial help. Stratton nodded again. But he did not ask his secretary to write out the check. Still, the agent knew that he had presented the case well. Stratton was clearly impressed. Stratton's check would turn up in the morning mail.

It didn't. Instead the agent and everyone else in the United States read that Winfield Stratton had come out for the silver maniac, William Jennings Bryan. He placed on deposit at the Springs First National Bank $100,000 in cash to be bet on Bryan if

someone was willing enough to bet $300,000 on
McKinley.

News of this bet nearly crowded McKinley
and Bryan off the nation's front pages. It was the
largest bet ever offered by one man on an election.
And to most people it seemed as odd an act as a man
could commit. Why, if Bryan won the election and the
United States resumed silver coinage at 16-to-1,
Stratton's gold wealth would be cut in half!

A group of reporters asked Stratton to explain
himself. He gave each of them a slip of paper containing these words:

"I do not make the offer because of any information that I have on the election but I have a feeling
that Bryan is going to win. I am deeply interested in
seeing Bryan elected. I realize that the maintenance of
the gold standard would perhaps be best for me indi-
vidually but I believe that free silver is the best thing
for the working masses of this country.

It is because I have a great respect for the
intelligence and patriotism of the working people that

I am willing to make such an offer."

The dignity and sincerity of Stratton's statement thrilled the country and sent a chill down the spines of the Republican managers. Up to then, McKinley's election seemed as sure as Christmas. Now the Republicans had serious qualms. To counteract Stratton's statement, campaign officials came out with all sorts of absurd whistlings in the dark. They declared that Stratton's bet could be covered fifty times.

Nobody did cover it. Stratton had scared the daylights out of every rich man in the Republican Party. The Democrats jeered and took tremendous heart. Their renewed spirit almost accomplished the impossible. McKinley just did squeak through with 7,100,000 votes against Bryan's 6,500,000.

During these years, Stratton associated mainly with old friends of his carpentry and prospecting days. An exception was handsome and mercurial

Verner Reed. From the time of the Portland fight Stratton had kept in touch with Reed, now age 33. Reed seemed to attract romantic experiences. He had roamed extensively in New Mexico and had become popular among the Indian tribes there. Stratton loved Reed's tale of how he nearly died once trying to endure a four-day bear dance with an iron-muscled Indian maiden. Stratton fell into a habit of telling Reed secrets about the Independence Mine that only his own foremen knew. He discussed the running value of assays, the average monthly profit, the estimated worth of hundreds of pillars left in stopes to support the underground. One day Reed swung gaily into Stratton's office wearing a brand-new tweed suit and matching cap. He was off to Europe. He said he wanted to see if European maidens could dance as well as those in New Mexico. To pay his expenses he would open offices in London and Scotland for the sale of Cripple Creek stocks.

Some weeks later Reed wrote Stratton that business was slow because Europeans were interested in the gold of the South African Transvaal. But he had met John Hays Hammond, the great American engineer. Hammond had just paid a fine of $125,000 to the Boers for his part in the Jamestown Raid. He had been handling Cecil Rhodes' Transvaal properties but he was not loved in the Rand now and he had joined a London investment company called Venture Corporation.

Reed's next letter explained how he perceived bit by bit that Hammond was more intrigued by Cripple than he pretended to be. He was probably worried by the Transvaal political situation and its threat to English properties. What Hammond needed was a spectacular gold mine elsewhere, the stocks of which could be sold to British investors if things went badly in South Africa. At each interview with Hammond, Reed dropped nuggets of inside information about the Independence. Hammond picked them up. Before long, Reed wrote Stratton of his strong suspicion that Hammond wanted the Independence for the Venture Corporation.

When Reed came home to visit he met T.A. Rickard, state geologist for Colorado, in Stratton's office. Rickard had been examining the Kalgoorlie gold camp in Western Australia. He told Reed and Stratton that John Hays Hammond had cabled him for data on the merits of Kalgoorlie and Cripple Creek, Rickard replied that Cripple had Kalgoorlie beat hollow. He added that Stratton's Independence was the most promising mine he had ever seen.

When Rickard left the office, Reed asked Stratton to sell the Independence to the Venture Corporation. Stratton said absolutely no. Reed laid a $50 bill on the desk before Stratton. Would Stratton bet fifty that he would not agree to sell the Independence? Stratton, smiling, placed his fifty beside Reed's. Then Reed told Stratton that he could get a fairly good price for the Independence if Stratton would give Reed an option. Stratton answered that the sort of money he would require for his dream mine hardly fitted Reed's phrase, "a fairly good price." To seal the doom of Reed's foolish bet, Stratton said slyly," Verner, I wouldn't take $5,000,000 for the Independence!"

Reed murmured, "How about $10,000,000?"

Stratton felt faint. No wonder. From Reed's past performances, Stratton knew that if Reed mentioned 10 million he could get 10 million. And what was $10,000,000 in the '90's? It was ten times as much money as you could possibly imagine. Income taxes did not exist. Most things cost a fifth of what they cost now. The equivalent today would be $50,000,000.

Stratton heard himself saying, "Yes, I'll take ten million."

When Reed left Stratton he had in his hand two $50 bills and an option to sell the Independence.

Reed returned to England. He haunted Hammond. The price of the Independence to the Venture Corporation was not 10 but 11 million since Reed placed a modest value of $1,000,000 on his services. In the summer of '98 Reed mentioned to Hammond for the first time the $11,000,000 figure. Hammond declared himself totally uninterested in the Independence even at a sane price. Reed watched the critical state of affairs in the Transvaal. He bided his time.

One day Hammond asked Reed for a report on the Independence. Reed cabled T.A. Rickard whom Hammond knew well. Stratton spent a week taking Rickard through the Independence underground. Rickard cabled Hammond that ore worth $7,000,000 was sitting around in the Independence stopes waiting to be hauled away. The mine was only 900 feet deep! Stratton's books showed that he had removed ore valued at $3,837,360 for a net profit of $2,402,164. This profit of 63 percent showed that the ore was incredibly rich.

Reed let Rickard's report simmer in Hammond's mind. He knew that Hammond was used to mining at depths of a mile and more. The Independence vein might extend down at least a mile. If an ignorant carpenter could take out a fortune, John Hays Hammond could do a hundred times better. In March of '99 Reed applied pressure. Reed and Hammond both knew that war was imminent in the Transvaal. The Rand mines would have to close. Reed told Hammond to buy the Independence at $11,000,000 or else. Hammond bleated pathetically. Reed's price was outrageous. Hammond would buy Tom Walsh's Camp Bird at Ouray instead. Reed knew how weak that bluff was. The Camp Bird in '99 wasn't half the mine the Independence was.

And so Hammond gave in. Reed cabled Stratton that he was worth $10,000,000 more. Stratton sailed for London. He was feeling wretched and he took his doctor along to treat his diabetes and liver trouble which Stratton aggravated by continuing his quart-a-day whiskey ration. Stratton signed final papers with the Venture Corporation. It was the biggest gold deal in history. And the brilliant mining experts got stung by the carpenter. Time would prove that Hammond paid far too much for the Independence. It earned only $5,237,739 during the next sixteen years before being sold to the Portland for $350,000.

After his London visit, Stratton took treatments in Carlsbad and Vienna. His interpreter was his Swiss bootmaker, Bob Schwarz. He and Bob called on Bob's sister in Switzerland. Stratton bought the sister a home and handled her an envelope when he left. Inside she found $20,000. In Paris, Stratton was pestered by reporters and by stunning, impoverished princesses of various colors seeking matrimony. Spring tourists were there in force burning up Cripple Creek profits. He met Jimmy Burns' sisters who were buying Catholic altar pieces. At the Café de la Paix he met Sam Strong almost buried among cocottes.

He crossed the Seine to visit Verner Reed in his Montparnasse studio. Reed was busy painting a beautiful nude girl. He wore a green velvet jacket and a black string tie. Reed introduced him to the nude model who stepped toward him to shake his hand. Stratton mumbled. "Pleased to meet you," and tried in panic to back away from the bare flesh. Reed made him sit down. The girl slipped on a smock and the three drank *café au lait.* Verner told Stratton he had salted away his million-dollar commission. Having reached the ripe old age of 36, he had decided to retire and spend the rest of his life in pleasant Bohemian pursuit of the arts. Actually Reed stood Paris only ten years. Then he came home to make $20,000,000 in Wyoming oil.

Carlsbad and Vienna did Stratton no good. He

got home in worse health than ever. His spirit was sick too. Events at Cripple distressed him. He saw signs everywhere that the camp was being degraded by the money-greed of its people. Money, for instance, was destroying the lifelong friendship between Jimmy Burns and Jimmy Doyle. Stratton had observed months earlier that the two small Irishmen were on the outs. Burns had descended one morning in the Anna Lee shaft of the Portland group to inspect stopes. When he returned to the surface eight miners entered the cage. As the cage went down, a pillar crumbled in a stope somewhere. The mountain sank, the shaft vanished and the eight men were crushed instantly.

It was Cripple's greatest disaster. Burns, anguished, spent $100,000 recovering the bodies which were mashed almost beyond recognition. He spent a larger sum compensating the families of the dead miners. As a result the Portland Company had no money for the March dividend. Jimmy Doyle hinted that Burns was negligent in letting the men go down in the Anna Lee. Burns had an Irish fit and resigned as president of the Portland. He declared that maybe 28-year-old Doyle could run the mine better if he had time to leave his favorite pool hall.

S tratton calmed Burns and Doyle down. He induced Burns to resume the presidency. But he seldom saw the old friends together thereafter. Burns was preoccupied with piling up money, improving his social graces and being a provisional member of the El Paso Club. Doyle just wanted to be popular as mayor of the wide-open town of Victor which had grown up on Wilson Creek. The big break came in November of '98. Doyle sued Burns for $700,000 worth of alleged Portland property which he claimed Burns had withheld from him. The Portland was incorporated in Iowa so Doyle sued in an Iowa court. Burns went to a Colorado Springs judge and got an injunction restraining Doyle from pressing the suit. Doyle ignored it and won a $700,000 judgment against Burns. This Iowa judgment made Doyle guilty of contempt as far as the Springs judge was concerned. He ordered Doyle to refuse the Iowa judgment or go to jail.

Stratton begged Burns and Doyle to make up. He reminded them of their early struggles on Battle Mountain, of the lawsuits they had won. He enlisted the help of Burns' sisters who loved both men. The feud went on. Doyle moved to Denver beyond the jurisdiction of the Springs court. Stratton concluded that he would never return to El Paso County. But Doyle did return and voluntarily entered the county jail. He told newsmen that he would rot in prison before he would give in to Burns.

He rotted for seven months, sulking in his cell, smoking stogies, issuing blasts at the ex-plumber. In March of '99, Doyle's followers elected him for this third term as Mayor of Victor. In June, Doyle charged that Burns was trying to blow him up with nitroglycerin cartridges which some children found on the jail's cellar steps. He asserted also that Burns was getting richer on illegal railroad and milling rebates. James Ferguson Burns said nothing at all. Finally the courts got together. The Iowa court set aside Doyle's

$700,000 judgment against Burns. The Springs court dropped the contempt charge against Doyle.

After 209 days in jail, Jimmy Doyle was freed. He was carried in triumph to Victor where he was given a beer-and-pretzel reception bigger than that given William Jennings Bryan three weeks earlier.

Burns and Doyle had become bitter enemies because of money. And money, which Winfield Stratton possessed by the bale, was making his own life miserable. J. Maurice Finn, an old friend who had helped him round out the Independence property, was a Stratton specialist now. If anyone wanted to try to squeeze some money out of the old Midas, Finn was the lawyer to hire. Leslie Popejoy sued him for half his property, claiming Stratton had defrauded him of his grubstake interest by belittling the Independence. Stratton could have beaten Popejoy easily but he felt sorry for the plasterer. He paid him $40,000 and Popejoy withdrew the suit.

One suit really hurt Stratton. Candace Root brought it. For years he had had a paternal tenderness for Candace which he expressed by giving her money when her alcoholism became acute. Candace's beauty was gone now. Her appealing air of gentle confusion was now the vacant stare of the sot. She sued Stratton for $200,000, alleging breach of promise to marry. Candace testified that Stratton had lured her into his bed unfairly at his Wilson Creek cabin and had got her pregnant. Stratton denied luring her, unfairly or otherwise. He told the court that it was no trick to get Candace into bed. Everyone in Cripple had observed her losing her virtue profitably since '92 and why should she blame her pregnancy on him particularly?

The case was dismissed. As Stratton rose to leave the court, Candace threw her arms around him and wept. He gave her some bills and asked her not to betray him again.

The virus of money-love was really an epidemic. One aspect was the gangsterism directed by Grant and Sherman Crumley. Their projects included robbing trains, holding up express wagons, counterfeiting rail passes and rolling drunks. Stratton learned further that the Crumleys had originated high-grading, or the theft of rich ore. This practice was adopted by hundreds of miners who robbed their employers of at least a million dollars annually by chipping ore from rich veins. A handful of high-grade ore might be worth several dollars. The miners would hide it in shoe tops or secret pockets or in bags between their legs. Some of them parked sacks of it in worked-out drifts and returned for it at night. The stolen ore was sold through a system of fences. The high-graders would hand the packages to a bartender or cigar clerk or a laundryman. An assayer would collect them and remove the gold in his small chlorination plant. He would pay each miner for his gold at the rate of $10 an ounce, or half the official rate.

High-grading, of course, was plain stealing. Stratton pointed this out to friends who were engaged in the business. They merely shrugged. Stratton didn't understand. Everyone was high-grading. It wasn't dishonest any more. Collection plates at Sunday church were cluttered with it. The minister handed it to the crooked assayer after church. Young men were paying for their college education by high-grading in summer. Bank officials bought huge amounts of stolen gold. Mine executives cooperated with ore thieves, thereby robbing their own stockholders of profits.

Cripple Creek gold!

Then came the tragedy of Sam Strong. And this time, as before, the cause was money.

Burly, truculent Sam was not a favorite of Stratton's. Even in his carpentering days when Sam brought lumber to him from Newton's, Stratton thought he was too crude and too loud. But he liked Sam for old times' sake. They had gone through a lot during their first discouraging year on Battle Mountain. Sam was a good fellow at heart. He might have lived a decent life under ordinary circumstances. His bad luck began when he found the Strong Mine and went on to make a million.

Sam had three classic weaknesses—liquor, women and gambling. He couldn't indulge them as a poor man. His gold changed that. The richer he got the more he drank and gambled. And the more he exercised his sex appeal. Soon he was tangled up with so many women that he married one in self-defense. She was a gentle, admirable girl named Regina Neville, age 19. Sam was 38.

Just after the wedding, a process server ordered Sam to appear in a $250,000 breach of promise suit brought by Miss Luella Vance of Goldfield. Luella said that $250,000 was the "sum necessary to alleviate her lacerated feelings and suffering which she sustains by the loss of Mr. Strong's companionship and to make her life worth living." Then came a second summons. Nellie Lewis, Sam's old mistress, demanded $200,000, adding that Sam had been promising to marry her since '93—every time he had taken her to New York for a whirl, in fact. Poor Sam and Regina slipped off to Paris to let the hail of suits abate. On their return, Sam spent half a million getting clear. Nellie Lewis was awarded $50,000. Luella Vance settled out of court for another $50,000.

Through Sam's troubles Regina stood by staunchly and even kept him sober. Afterward he hit the bottle harder than ever. He had many enemies. And he still had too much money. The most fervent of his enemies was Grant Crumley. Grant hated Sam in general. He also hated him in particular because Sam ran up a gambling debt of $2,500 at Grant's Newport Saloon and paid him by check. Next day Sam stopped the check, claiming Grant's wheel was crooked. A week later he settled with Grant for $200.

Soon after, Sam went on a tour of the Bennett Avenue gambling houses with Regina's father, John Neville. They played at Johnny Nolon's until after midnight. Then they ambled a block east to Newport. Neville pleaded with Sam to go home. Sam wanted to gamble. He moved through the Newport bar into the gambling room. By 5:30 a.m., when the town of Mount Pisgah was yellow with the rising sun, Sam was ahead $140 at roulette.

Grant Crumley looked in from the bar. Sam shouted, "Whatsa matter, Grant? You don't happen to be running a straight wheel for a change?"

Grant withdrew. Sam staggered off to the toilet. Neville went to the bar to talk to Crumley who mentioned the $2,500 check Sam had stopped. Sam, coming to the bar, caught the gist of the talk. He yelled to Grant, "Here, that's my daddy you're talking to!"

Grant apologized. As he did so, he removed his arm from the cigar counter on which he was leaning and put both hands in his pockets. Sam poured himself some wine. Suddenly he dropped his glass, drew his revolver and yelled, "Take your hands out of your pockets, Crumley, or I'll kill you!"

Neville pressed in to restrain Sam. Crumley ducked behind the bar screen next to the cigar counter. He emerged from the screen with a sawed-off shotgun which he held across the bar two feet from Sam's head. Sam was so surprised that he dropped his revolver. The explosion of Crumley's gun rocked the room. The No. 4 buckshot made a jagged hole above Sam's right eye. He died at 8 a.m.

Some months later Grant Crumley was acquitted of murder on the grounds of self-defense.

When Stratton heard about Sam he left his Pikes Peak Avenue office and walked tiredly home. He drew the shades in the parlor, lay down on the couch and called for his whisky. He lay there drinking for a week. The bout settled nothing. Even as he drank he grew richer by $20,000. He was being crushed by the weight of his money. If he were to survive its evils he would have to unload some of it somehow.

For Christmas presents that year he gave $50,000 to each of his key employees. He bought half a dozen homes for other employees. He gave $5,000 to the discoverer of Cripple Creek, Bob Womack. The old cowboy, forgotten and penniless, had a job delivering laxatives for a drugstore. Stratton sent 13-year-old Louis Persinger to Germany to study violin (Louis became one of America's best violin teachers). He gave Colorado Springs the ground on which the city hall stands. He bought El Paso County courthouse so that the county could build a new one. He bought the present post-office block and gave it to the government for half its cost. He built a five-story building for the Colorado Springs Mining Exchange.

He bought the dilapidated Springs streetcar system and made it one of the finest in the world at a cost of $1,500,000. At the Cheyenne Mountain end of the streetcar line he built a public park with a bandstand. He paid for free concerts at the park on Sundays.

He paid his dues five years ahead as a member of the carperters' union.

He bought $2,000,000 worth of Denver real estate, including a $650,000 mortgage on the Brown Palace Hotel. He did not, as the fable goes, buy this mortgage because he and a drunken blonde had been refused a room by Manager Maxcy Tabor. There was no drunken blonde. If there had been one, or even a dozen, Maxcy would have welcomed them with open arms into the Brown. Hadn't Stratton torn up the $15,000 note of Maxcy's father when Horace Tabor was down and out?

Altogether Stratton unloaded $4,500,000 in four months. But he was making little headway. He hadn't touched the 10 million which he was receiving from the sale of the Independence. What he needed was a project on which he could really splurge. Perhaps he had had that project in the back of his mind all along. For years he had brooded over the notion that Cripple was created by the mushrooming of volcanic blowouts. He had amused himself by charting the slant of Cripple's big veins. He decided that they converged in depth. They must meet a mile of so down. That meeting point must contain ore infinitely richer than any other ore found to date.

His charts indicated that the center of this Pandora's Box lay beneath a claim called the Plymouth Rock near the top of Ironclad Hill. Even before he sold the Independence, Stratton had bought claims near the Plymouth Rock. Now he increased purchases until he was spending $10,000 every day. Soon he owned 100 claims with a surface area of 600 acres in the exact center of the camp. Many of the prices paid were inflated by his own impatient buying. His total outlay came to $7,000,000. In addition he was spending more than a million a year on development.

Such spending had a wonderful effect on the economy of Cripple Creek and of Colorado Springs. The magic word was Stratton, Stratton, Stratton! His development crew numbered 600 men, which was a fifth of Cripple's entire labor force. People discussed him incessantly—on the electric cars, in the churches and schools, in the saloons and parlor houses. As a mark of appreciation, members of the Colorado Springs Mining Exchange voted to give Stratton a great banquet. They worked on the affair for weeks. Chester Alan Arthur, gourmet son of the ex-President, was delegated to make the menu and choose the wines. One hundred and sixty people attended, including General Palmer and ex-Governor Adams. Sixteen speakers praised the ex-carpenter. Thunderous applause for him went far into the night.

The only trouble was that the guest of honor failed to show up.

Stratton had meant to go. Jimmy Burns, a Mining Exchange officer, had come to this house to help him into evening clothes. Stratton had never worn such duds before. Jimmy was explaining the mysteries of shirt studs when Stratton moved off from him a few steps. He examined Burns. He noted the beautiful cut of Jimmy's narrowing trousers with their wide satin stripe. He saw Jimmy's elegant patent leather shoes, the graceful white vest, white tie and wing collar. He saw Jimmy's pink face glowing with happiness, his neatly trimmed mustache, his white hair parted in the exact middle.

"Jimmy," Stratton said as he began taking off his new stiff shirt. "I'm not going. Tell 'em I'm sick. Tell 'em anything. I don't belong in that crowd. It's all right for you. It's what you want and it suits you. I'm proud of you, Jimmy! Now get along to the banquet and enjoy yourself. Me, I'm going to have a drink."

It was nice of people to show their gratitude. Stratton did receive some pleasure out of it. But the pleasure did not compensate him for the miseries he endured as the penalty of being rich. Every day brought dozens of crank letters. On the short walk from his Weber Street home to his office he would be stopped a dozen times by strangers begging for money. If he gave them money or even spoke to these strangers he was apt to find himself hauled into court on some fake charge. And then there was the responsibility. He was merely a man and yet he had at his disposal the power to make or break hundreds of men and women. Their lives depended on his whims to hear them tell it.

One day a young man hit pay dirt on Bull Hill and was offered a good price for his claim. He wrote Stratton for advice. Should he sell his claim or hang on to it as Stratton had done, hoping for millions in the end? Stratton replied:

"If you get a chance to sell your property for $100,000 do it. I once gave an option on the Independence and a thousand times I have wished that the holder had taken it up. Too much money is not good for any man. I have too much and it is not good for me. A hundred thousand dollars is as much money as the man of ordinary intelligence can take care of. Large wealth has been the ruin of many a young man."

As Stratton's spirit despaired, his thin body grew weaker. Now in 1902 he was almost an invalid. His years of alcoholism had caused dietary deficiencies which resulted in a diseased liver. He gave himself over to his doctor and his nurses. He hid in his curtained home. He read and slept and fretted and drank two quarts of whisky each day. He was visited occasionally by paid women from Denver but he was beyond physical pleasure. He was only in his early fifties and yet he felt a thousand years old. He looked empty, finished. The cords stood out on the back of his neck.

He speculated often on why the joy and zest of life had left him. His dislike of being rich explained it only partly. Surely he wasn't being punished for his sins. He wasn't a bad man. He had worked hard and faithfully always. He had been honest and kindly. The only act he had ever been ashamed of was taking that pot shot at his father when he was 12. He had, true enough, drunk too much whisky and enjoyed loose women. But his conduct was normal for his place and time.

What then was the matter?

One day Stratton had the answer.

His troubles started when he found the big Independence vein in '93. That vein was his pot of gold at the end of the rainbow which he had chased contentedly for seventeen years all over Colorado's mountains. Finding the vein had brought him to the end of everything that had made his life really worth living. Most people were lucky because life for them wasn't just one big quest as his had been but a succession of little quests. Jimmy Burns always had one ahead. After he got elected foreman of Hook and Ladder company No. 1 in '88 he went on to make good at Cripple and to win and discard Georgia Hayden and to become a member of the El Paso Club and to buy a great home in the North End. Recently he had built a third railroad to the gold camp and he married the most beautiful girl in St. Joseph, Missouri. Now he was thinking of the children he would have and was making inquiries about eastern colleges for their education.

Stratton had tried to emulate Jimmy. He had tried to create a new quest for himself. He had spent $8,000,000 on the Pandora's Box idea around the Plymouth Rock. So far not one of those 100 claims showed promise but that wasn't the worst of it. The project just wasn't a genuine quest. It was make-believe, he finally admitted to himself.

It would, Stratton concluded, be good to die. And soon. He was ready. He had made his will. And he got some small pleasure thinking about one item in that will. It would astonish people. And it would put his mind at rest about having tried to kill his father, Myron Stratton. When you want to die badly it doesn't take long. Stratton wasted away through the spring and summer of 1902. His infected liver did not cause him much pain. On Saturday, September 13, 1902, he went into a coma. Sunday evening Bob Schwarz sat with him in the quiet Weber Street house. Stratton roused briefly and asked Bob how his sister was getting along in Switzerland.

He died at 9:35 p.m.

Next day he was eulogized throughout Colorado. On Tuesday his body lay in state at his Mining Exchange and 9,000 people filed by. At 2 p.m. his streetcars stopped for five minutes. On Wednesday he was buried at Evergreen Cemetery on a wooded knoll facing Pikes Peak.

He had been the first of many Colorado Springs residents to make a million dollars at Cripple Creek. He was the first of these millionaires to wind up at Evergreen.

Winfield Stratton's will was read a week later. As had been expected he left a million dollars to various nieces and nephews and to the son of Zeurah Stewart. But the main bequest had not been expected at all. Its unique provisions encouraged a hundred people to jump in and try to break the will. Twelve women appeared claiming to be Stratton's widows. The State of Colorado claimed the estate on grounds that the will's trustees were incompetent. Leslie Popejoy sued again for half of Stratton's properties.

The surprise bequests assigned $6,000,000 of the estate to establish an institution for the care of children and old people. It was to be called the Myron Stratton Home. And it was the thought of this home that had given Stratton some comfort in his last days. It wasn't to be just another rich man's charity. It would have no equal for beauty and peace anywhere in the world. Orphans would be reared with the same advantages enjoyed by children of the well-to-do. Old people would have no feeling of living in an institution. They would have individual cottages just as if they were in their own homes.

Stratton's trustees defeated every attempt to break the will. And so the Myron Stratton Home was built. Today its stately buildings, its lawns and bowers, its swimming pool and tennis courts and playing fields, its curving avenues of neat homes, sit on land near the Cheyenne Mountain trail over which Stratton led his burro in '91. The home cares for 100 children and 100 old people on a budget of $200,000 annually. The money is earned by the business properties in Colorado Springs and Denver which Stratton bought in the 90's. The home must come very close to Stratton's dream of it. Many of the old people there must know the happiness that Stratton could not manage for himself in his last years.

The flags of Cripple Creek went to half-staff on the day of Stratton's death. In the following weeks the lusty, gusty, seemingly indestructible gold camp began to understand what he had meant to it. There was a flood of bankruptcies. Dozens of great mines closed down. Financiers moved in to begin the consolidations which Stratton had feared and which would transform the independent camp into an unromantic big business. As the financiers moved in, Cripple's colorful personalities moved out. Johnny Nolon, Grant Crumley and other gamblers went to greener pastures in Nevada. Hazel Vernon and Lola Livingston returned to Denver. Myers Avenue's pretty sporting women left the field to the hags. Standards of morality toppled. From then on Myers was a place where every man had to look out for himself.

Gold camp production figures for 1902 would show that it was the last year of boom production— $19,000,000 worth of gold. In 1903 Cripple's production slumped to $13,000,000.

When Winfield Stratton died on September 14, 1902, the best part of the world's greatest gold camp died with him.